SMALL GROUP

ToolBox

STRONG FAITH

FOR TOUGH TIMES

Ron Kallmier

CONTENTS

PREFACE

'Faith' tends to be a fuzzy concept in our culture. As it is an abstract term used by different groups of people in different ways, this fuzziness is not surprising. Nevertheless it is important that those of us who follow Jesus Christ have a clear picture of what the New Testament teaches on this essential characteristic of Christian living.

Hebrews chapters 11 and 12 contain extensive teaching on the topic of faith so it is a good place for us to start our discovery. We will return to the teaching in these two chapters from time to time because they contain such a rich resource for our studies, but we will begin by highlighting a few key insights that we find in the first few verses.

> *What is faith? It is the confident assurance that what we hope for is going to happen. It is the evidence of things we cannot yet see. God gave his approval to people in days of old because of their faith. By faith we understand that the entire universe was formed at God's command, that what we now see did not come from anything that can be seen. It was by faith that Abel brought a more acceptable offering to God than Cain did. God accepted Abel's offering to show that he was a righteous man. And although Abel is long dead, he still speaks to us because of his faith. It was by faith that Enoch was taken up to heaven without dying – "suddenly he disappeared because God took him." But before he was taken up, he was approved as pleasing to God. So, you see, it is impossible to please God without faith. Anyone who wants to come to him must believe that there is a God and that he rewards those who sincerely seek him.*
> (Heb. 11:1–6)

When we examine these profound words more closely what do we find?
- Our faith is a delight to God
- We may not experience or see some of the results of our faith in our lifetime
- Faith is often rewarded in ways beyond our wildest dreams
- Faith has pleasing God as its highest aim
- A living faith must be founded firmly on God's unfailing faithfulness towards us.

Faith always looks beyond our current changing circumstances to the unchanging faithfulness of God Himself. This is beautifully expressed in Lamentations 3:22–26:

> The unfailing love of the LORD never ends! By his mercies we have been kept from complete destruction. Great is his faithfulness; his mercies begin afresh each day. I say to myself, "The LORD is my inheritance; therefore, I will hope in him!" The LORD is wonderfully good to those who wait for him and seek him. So it is good to wait quietly for salvation from the LORD.

For Christians, faith should become an essential thread woven seamlessly through the fabric of our entire lives. Of course the crucial point is that we understand what this thing called *faith* is and are clear about what it means for us to live the faith-filled, satisfying life that God intends for us.

These small group sessions explore four familiar elements of a Christian's faith journey – Faith Foundations; Faith Builders; Faith Challenges; Faith Benefits. The aim of these four study sessions is to help each of us build a faith that not only survives but also thrives through the inevitable joys and trials of normal living. My prayer is that your understanding of faith will be enriched and your walk with our Lord Jesus Christ will be more confident and rewarding as a result.

Ron Kallmier, 2013

SUGGESTIONS FOR USING THIS STUDY GUIDE

SUGGESTIONS FOR GROUP LEADERS

- As far as possible keep discussions practically orientated, including the Bible study section each week.

- Many of the suggestions for individuals and groups are quite 'meaty' and you may find that you only cover one of these during a group session. This is OK.

- Encourage the group members to do some preparation for the following week. Their best preparation may be as simple as thinking over how they respond to the questions or issues featured in each study.

- Some Christians think of faith as mostly to do with what they believe, but the scriptural view is much more expansive than this. One aim of this series is to become aware that faith, biblically speaking, engages every part of our human nature.

- The group times will be the most effective if there is integrity and honesty in the discussion. It is the leader who will be the best example and best encourager in facilitating openness among group participants.

- There are four parts to each of the studies in this book. First, the 'Preview' provides an introduction to the set topic. Next, 'Personal Exploration' offers an individual focus, guiding personal study and reflection. Third, 'Studying Together' contains questions and suggestions for discussing the key Bible passages within a small group context. Finally, 'Applying the Scriptures' raises some thought-provoking questions about faith in everyday life.

- Of course, you are free to use the suggestions in any way that best fits your own group. While the book is designed to be covered in four small group sessions you may find it helpful to use some of the suggestions, discard others and add your own too. You may prefer to use the 'Preview' for each session as an alternative way of stimulating discussion when your group meets.

- It is recommended that you address **real questions** and **real issues** from within the group whenever this is appropriate. Sessions are not intended to be merely a theoretical discussion, but should be very practical.

- In a healthy group environment, positive experiences and any uncertainties or concerns of group members will surface. This openness will stimulate frank and open exploration of the issues raised.

- Ideally, group members should complete the study series with a clearer understanding of the nature of faith and more awareness of their own faith strengths and growth areas.

- By the way, we suggest you don't pressure anyone to contribute to the discussion if they appear unwilling. Everyone should be given the opportunity to speak; but also, make space for individuals to process their own thoughts and to consider what is being said by others.

SUGGESTIONS FOR YOUR PERSONAL USE

- This study series aims to apply biblical experiences and teaching to the everyday life experiences of individual Christians.

- In addition to the spaces provided in this study book, you may find it useful to get hold of a small journal or notebook to use while you are focusing on this topic. Here are some things you may like to jot down:

  - Your personal understanding and experiences of walking by faith with God.
  - Ways in which people in the Bible displayed their faith in God as they responded to His call.
  - Any reliable experiences of other Christians whose stories shed some light on what it means to walk by faith.
  - Questions you may have or ideas you would like to bring to your group.

SUGGESTIONS FOR SMALL GROUPS

- To set the direction that this study book takes, it is recommended that every group member reads the 'Introduction', preferably before the first session or at least during the first session.

- If you plan to use the book in a small group, it is recommended that all group members read the 'Preview' section and spend some time in personal preparation for the next group meeting. With our busy lives this may be quite a challenge, but the preparation will help to give maximum benefit to all group members.

- Because each Christian's life story is unique, it should not be surprising if we have differing views about what faith is and how we are meant to live faithfully in our day to day lives. It is important that everyone is heard and understood respectfully. Each person's perspective should be appreciated, even when it is not that of other people in the group.

- We can all learn from one another, even from those of us who have serious doubts or questions. In our discussions we will need to turn to the Scriptures as our primary authority and source of our information on this topic.

- Because living as followers of Jesus Christ in today's world is often challenging, especially for those of us in circumstances where our Christian commitment and beliefs are challenged or ridiculed, my prayer is that your private study and your shared times together will strengthen and encourage you.

INTRODUCTION

What is faith?

How would you answer this question? No doubt there are many views among Christians about what the word 'faith' means. And probably there are even more questions concerning this topic. Nevertheless, faith is a central teaching of Jesus and of the Bible as a whole. It is a very important quality for each of us because the substance and strength of our faith will determine whether we stand or fall in those pressure seasons of our lives. As we work through the sessions we will endeavour to unpack the richness of this concept of faith – a quality that is so essential to effective Christian living.

There are many possible starting points for our exploration, but to begin our journey in this series we will turn to Matthew 14:22–36. This is an account of the disciples in a storm–swept boat at night, in Galilee. Jesus drew close to them, walking on the raging waters. This traumatic incident provides us with so many insights into the complex nature of faith and highlights what a lack of faith looks like. What becomes clear in this powerful story is that our faith (or our lack of faith) touches every area of our humanity.

Faith and our human spirit

At its core, our faith is a spiritual matter. It has at its centre our relationship with God. Spiritually speaking, faith can be described as a matter of **trust** – a crucial element in any healthy relationship. The opposite of faith at a spiritual and relational level is **distrust** – a character flaw that came to the surface in all the disciples except Peter, at least for a time. Their basic distrust was obvious. These terrified men preferred the false security of their precarious boat to the risk of following Jesus' challenge to step out and walk to Him. Distrust is often behind our suspicious attitudes and cautious approach in our relationships with other people. This response may be understandable if another person has hurt an individual in the past. Distrust in God, however, imprisons us within our own limited capacities. It reduces our freedom.

Faith and our emotions

From this story we learn that faith also has an emotional element. Emotionally, faith shows itself in an **inner calmness** or **confident assurance** even in the seasons of life's worst trials. Jesus gives us the ultimate picture of this calmness in His trial before Pontius Pilate (John 18:28–38). At an emotional level the opposite response to faith is **fear**. Fear becomes **terror** in its extreme form. It was terror that overwhelmed the disciples' emotions (vv25–26) not only because of the threat of imminent disaster in the storm but also because of the ghost-like appearance of Jesus on the raging sea.

Faith and our thinking

What does faith look like at a rational or thinking level? Essentially it can be detected in a **well-founded** and **confident belief**. Its antithesis is **doubt**. It is important to realise that what we think has a dominating influence on both our emotions and on our behaviour. The disciples saw a human shape where none should be, walking on the top of troubled waters no less. Their thinking led them to conclude this had to be a ghost. Consequently, this false perception increased their terror and left them frozen by fear, huddling in their water-filled boat. Can we blame them? Would we have done differently? Fear does that. It reduces our capacity for healthy, positive action by immobilising us and diminishing our God-given potential for positive action. Negative thoughts swirl around our minds when fear and doubt take over.

Faith and our actions

Faith also involves our *actions* and *behaviour*. James put it so well when he wrote in his letter: 'Dear brothers and sisters, what's the use of saying you have faith if you don't prove it by your actions? That kind of faith can't save anyone.' (For James's full comment on this point read James 2:14–26.) A faith that is simply a head belief or an emotional feel-good experience is not biblical faith. It is not the type of faith that Jesus Christ desires for us and demands of us. Living faith will express itself through our words, our hands and our feet. It demands action.

Bringing together the thoughts so far, we have noted that our faith involves **all** of who we are. This type of faith creates an inner assurance that God is trustworthy and caring. It leads us to put God's ideas and ways above our own. Our spirits, our thoughts, our emotions and our actions all become engaged in demonstrating our confidence in Him.

Faith is a grand adventure of trust in a faithful, loving God. We are able to engage in this adventure based on the strong foundations of the faith, hope and love that flow continuously from God to us (1 Cor. 13:13).

From the fragile seeds of our faith, God is willing and able to produce 'trees' for His own glory (Isa. 61:3), trees that are able to bear the necessary and very desirable fruit of His Holy Spirit:

> ... *when the Holy Spirit controls our lives, he will produce this kind of fruit in us: love, joy, peace, patience, kindness, goodness, faithfulness, gentleness, and self-control.*
> (Gal. 5:22–23)

PART ONE

FAITH FOUNDATIONS

PREVIEW

When you think about it, everyone has a measure of faith in his or her life. We sit on chairs believing they will hold us and eat food from the supermarkets not really being certain where it came from or how edible it is. We trust train drivers, bus drivers, taxi drivers and some of us even trust our lives into the hands of airline pilots, surgeons, dentists and fitness trainers. The list could go on of course.

What, then, is unique about the faith which we Christians discuss? First and foremost this faith has a focus – a central reference point for our lives, and this centre is a person, our Lord Jesus Christ. Essentially our faith rests in His claim to be the Son of God, come to earth to rescue His fallen creation. It is built upon the knowledge and experience of those who have travelled with Him before us and those who share our journey with us at this time.

As followers of Jesus Christ we believe that He is not only our focus but He is the source of our faith (He initiates it), and He is the ultimate fulfilment of all that our faith points us towards and all that we hope for (Heb. 12:1–2). It is through the power of the Holy Spirit that we can live by faith in Jesus no matter what life experiences come along.

> *So this is what the Sovereign Lord says: "See, I lay a stone in Zion, a tested stone, a precious* **cornerstone** *for a sure foundation; the one who trusts will never be dismayed."*
> (Isa. 28:16, NIV, emphasis mine)

Just living in a world of people and experiences, we learn to trust some people and not to trust others; to trust some things but not other things.

But the real question is, how much do we trust Jesus? In other words, how mature is our faith? How strong are our faith foundations?

Recently I have spent a considerable amount of time reflecting on the parable of the two builders, but rather than turning to Matthew's account (Matt. 7:24–29) I have been meditating on Luke's version (Luke 6:46–49). A number of Jesus' statements here captured my attention. First, to call Jesus Lord and not to do what He tells us to do is contradictory. We cannot have one without the other. Obedience to Him and faith in Him are strongly interrelated. Second, we are warned that our life foundation will be tested and unless the foundation is strong it will eventually fail. If our faith is actually in ourselves or something or someone else and not in Jesus Christ, we are building our lives on very shaky ground. God is not impressed with a religious show substituting for true faith. He examines our hearts, and as the writer of the letter to the Hebrews puts it: '… it is impossible to please God without faith' (Heb. 11:6).

This matter of our faith is serious business, but it leads to great personal satisfaction and blessings as the adventure of walking with God unfolds in our lives. He is always faithful.

REFLECTION
There is a beautiful expression of faith in Psalm 131. Take time to meditate on the visual imagery this short psalm contains.

PERSONAL EXPLORATION
It has been suggested that our faith involves our whole person – everything we are as an individual. Jesus emphasised that the greatest commandment is to: '... love the Lord your God with all your **heart**, all your **soul**, all your **strength**, and all your **mind**' (Luke 10:27, emphasis mine). The strength of our faith in God will be determined in part by our love for God.

1. What do you consider to be the strongest element of your faith – your **heart** (passion for God, your motivation or commitment to God), your **soul** (including will and emotions), your **mind** (including intellect) or your **physical strength** (faith in action)?

----

2. On reflection, do one or more of these faith elements need attention?

----

3. Which people have been the greatest positive influences on your faith? Why not take some time to recall their contribution in your own life and then give thanks to God for them.

----

4. Which two passages or verses from the Scriptures have encouraged your faith the most?

STUDYING TOGETHER

1. Hebrews 11:1–3

   Explore the key ideas concerning faith that these verses contain. What thoughts particularly impress individual group members in these words?

2. Hebrews 11:5–6

   What are the implications of the words, '… it is impossible to please God without faith'?

3. Hebrews 11

   This chapter has been described as the 'heroes of faith' chapter. Do you notice that there is no record of the sins or weaknesses of any of the people mentioned here? The cross truly has removed the record of our sins as far as the east is from the west. As an example of this, check out Moses (vv24–28); you will find some significant omissions and changes when compared with the account in Exodus 2–4. What implications do we discover for ourselves today?

4. Hebrews 12:1–4

What are some practical ways that we can look to Jesus, the champion who initiates and perfects our faith?

APPLYING THE SCRIPTURES

1. How would you describe the meaning of faith to someone who had never had any connection with Christians or Christianity?

2. Who were the most significant people in leading you into a life of faith in Jesus Christ? What was it about them that motivated you to become a follower of Jesus Christ?

3. Provide an opportunity for group members to tell their stories of how they found faith in Jesus Christ.

4. Discuss how your prayer, Bible reading, worship and/or Christian service have influenced your Christian faith.

_____

_____

_____

_____

_____

_____

_____

PART TWO

FAITH BUILDERS

PREVIEW

Why do some people appear to operate with greater faith than others? Is it to do with their personality, simply the way they were born, or does their level of faith derive from something else?

Jesus talked about the potential power of very little faith to achieve staggering things (Matt. 17:14–20), but then He said pointedly to His disciples that they did not have a sufficient level of faith for the task at hand. Clearly He expects that faith should develop and mature. And it follows that we can only achieve certain things if our faith has developed sufficiently. So how do we grow our faith?

At its very heart a stronger faith depends on a bigger view of God. A small 'God picture' will profoundly limit our ability to trust Him. Consequently we will not take those faith steps that lead us beyond our own capacity and our own vision of what is possible. In a number of seminars, reflecting on his own faith journey, John Wimber declared that 'faith' is spelt 'R–I–S–K'. This risk involves believing that God is as powerful and wise as the Scriptures say He is and that He loves us completely and unchangeably, even when what He asks us to do appears to be impossible.

Possibly you have longed for greater faith. You are not alone. The first disciples of Jesus felt exactly the same way.

One day the apostles said to the Lord, "We need more faith; tell us how to get it."

"Even if you had faith as small as a mustard seed," the Lord answered, "you could say to this mulberry tree, 'May God uproot you and throw you into the sea,' and it would obey you!"'

(Luke 17:5–6)

A greater faith and a more responsive obedience to God is not an optional extra. As we noted in the previous session, it is foundational for a highly effective and fulfilling Christian life. An important factor in developing an attitude of responsiveness to God is doing what Richard Blackaby has described as 'unlimiting God'. Here is a little of what he has to say:

> [1]*After many years of walking with God and seeking to go deeper with Him, I've drawn this conclusion:* **We** *limit God.* **We** *determine much of what we experience of God's power. And* **we** *set parameters on the depth of our relationship with God. In spite of limitless possibilities we choose to impede what God does in our lives, so that He must say to us, 'I spoke to you, rising up early and speaking, but you did not hear, and I called you, but you did not answer'* (Jer. 7:13, NKJV).

It should be clear then that a most important step in developing a greater level of faith is to seek to expand our view of God and His attitude towards us. The Scriptures are a profound source of information and inspiration for this task. Let's never forget that the angel said to Mary: '... nothing is impossible with God' (Luke 1:37).

But there are other ways of building our faith. We can learn from the faith adventures of other Christians. Books, DVDs and the Internet are a good source. And let's not overlook the stories of people we know or meet who can motivate us to take the 'RISK' of faith. God is truly bigger and more capable than you and I could ever imagine.

Some Christians find journalling their prayer requests and the answers to their prayers very beneficial. Reviewing their journal notes from time to time helps them to remember what God has done for them. As a result they are encouraged and their faith increases. It is too easy for us to forget the many ways in which God has intervened in our lives unless we make a conscious effort to use our memories and to be thankful.

It is important to be aware that a growing faith starts with little steps of obedience as we respond to the prompting of the Holy Spirit. We simply do the next thing that God puts in front of us. God calls us to have an adventure with Him by stepping out of the safety of our own little 'boats', whatever they may be. As we do, we become open to greater challenges.

[1] Blackaby, R, *Unlimited God* (Colorado Springs, Multnomah: 2008)

PERSONAL EXPLORATION

1. Think back on some times when you were keenly aware of God's activity in your life. If you keep a journal you may like to review what you have written. How did these events strengthen your faith?

2. Most of us have heard memorable stories of God's divine intervention. Which stand out in your mind? What impact have these stories had on your own faith?

3. Scriptural promises are powerfully inspiring for many Christians. Are there Bible passages that have helped to grow your faith?

4. Most of us have asked God for specific guidance at times. This guidance does not always come in ways that we expect, yet these experiences of His specific guidance become a positive faith-builder. What has been your own experience of this?

STUDYING TOGETHER

In this session's Bible discovery we will look at three of the people whom Hebrews 11 describes as examples of faith. After you read the passages, discuss what qualities earned each person the privilege of being called an example of faith. What can we learn from their examples? Are there any surprises here?

It is suggested that you spend most of your time on the number 4.

1. Noah: Hebrews 11:7

2. Sarah: Hebrews 11:11–12

3. Moses: Hebrews 11:24–28

4. Hebrew 11:13–16: What comments stand out to you in these verses? What picture of faith is painted in your mind?

APPLYING THE SCRIPTURES

1. Of all the characters mentioned in Hebrews 11, which one reminds you most of your own experience? Why did you choose this person?

2. Has there been a 'stand out' experience in your life that has strengthened your faith? How would you describe the impact of this event on you?

3. A stagnant relationship with God can never produce a stronger level of faith. Consider the current specific circumstances of each person in the group. What practical steps could you take in encouraging one another to become more sensitive to God's presence and His involvement in your lives?

_____

_____

_____

_____

_____

_____

_____

4. Any relationship takes time to develop and maintain. How can we maintain our awareness of God's unswerving faithfulness in the ups and downs of our busy lives?

_____

_____

_____

_____

_____

_____

_____

PART THREE

FAITH CHALLENGES

PREVIEW

A Christian life that is lived comfortably without any obvious need to trust God will be shallow. It will struggle to survive the trials that will inevitably come sooner or later. These trials are builders or breakers. They will either grow us or grind us. Many of the challenges to our faith are unwelcome, but faith that is not tested will never grow strong; never reach maturity. Untested faith will be a poor and weak imitation of what true faith in God is.

Faith challenges come across our lives in many shapes and forms, but they always involve our thought life in some way. Just as the first temptation was aimed at the mind (Gen. 3) so our greatest battles at some point will engage us in a conflict in our minds. Doubts and uncertainties can drain our faith reservoirs very quickly if we allow them to dominate us, especially if we rely on our reasoning alone.

It is in these seasons of struggle that we should turn to the encouragement of the Scriptures and also recall our former experiences of God's faithfulness. This will lead us successfully through any intellectual challenges with which we wrestle. Personally I found this approach to be very helpful in my early years when studying philosophy and psychology. Both these fields of university study attacked my Christian faith and beliefs head on. This is an important truth we noted in the Introduction of this study book. While the intellectual challenge was painful, the following year I knew that battle was over and my faith was now stronger than ever. I found a renewed peace of mind and was so pleased to realise that my faith does not rest on my intellectual capability alone.

Possibly your biggest faith challenges lies within you – negative self-talk, an enduring sense of unworthiness, dwelling on past sins and failures, feelings of inferiority, or reliving painful memories of the damage caused by others – these are common factors that may undermine our faith.

Because of this sense of inferiority we may feel that we are too bad, too weak, or too insignificant for God to love. As a consequence we may believe that He would not consider walking close to us or using us when it comes to doing something important for Him.

It may be that part of our problem is based on a perspective that people recorded in the Bible are superheroes. In reality, a closer look at the histories of these people of faith mentioned in Hebrews 11 makes it clear that they were fragile and failing people just like us. Despite their flaws and failings God still did remarkable things through them simply because they came to trust Him in spite of their waywardness and weaknesses. It is no different for us today.

God will use the trials that life brings our way to strengthen us if only we keep our focus on His goodness, His kindness and His love for us. If our faith is to grow, it is important that we learn to wait on God for His direction and His timing in the middle of the storms or the battles we face.

> *Do not throw away this confident trust in the Lord, no matter what*
> *happens. Remember the great **reward** it brings you!*
> (Heb. 10:35, emphasis mine)

> *Be still, and know that I am God; I will be exalted among the nations,*
> *I will be exalted in the earth.*
> (Psa. 46:10, NIV)

 ## PERSONAL EXPLORATION

For our personal consideration of the challenges to our faith, we turn back to the dynamic account of the disciples in the boat during the storm that we mentioned earlier. It is suggested you read through Matthew 14:22–36 a number of times, imagining yourself in the situation, and then consider the following questions. Record your thoughts and feelings as you do so.

1. Are you currently facing any testing experiences – the storms of life? How do you normally manage these events, emotionally and practically?

----

2. How aware are you of the presence of Jesus with you in these storms? What could you do to become more confident of His presence and help?

----

3. What steps of faith could you take now to prepare yourself for any future trials and difficulties?

----

4. Prayerfully invite Jesus 'into your own boat' – into any circumstances about which you are currently anxious.

STUDYING TOGETHER

There is a great integrity in the writings in the psalms. All the psalmists' thoughts and feelings are helpfully on display. The psalm of Asaph, Psalm 73, could have been written by some of us today and so it is the basis for our Bible study.

1. (vv1–14) What were some of the reasons that caused Asaph's faith to be in danger of failing?

----

2. Has anyone in the group experienced similar questions and doubts to those expressed by Asaph here? What were the circumstances that caused the challenge to your faith?

3. (vv15–20) What did Asaph realise that corrected his confused thinking and overcame his doubts?

4. (vv21–28) What was his emotional state during this time of uncertainty? What specific facts in his walk with God did he recall so that he was able to restore his faith in God's sovereignty and care?

APPLYING THE SCRIPTURES

1. What life experiences are the most challenging to your faith in God? How do you deal with these challenges?

2. Does God cause the faith challenges that come our way? Does He simply use whatever life brings across our path? Do you believe God uses both methods? Discuss your viewpoints and reasons.

3. We have noted that our faith challenges can either build or break our faith. Sometimes they simply move us to the side-lines. We go through the motions of being a disciple of Jesus Christ but we have very little personal connection with Him in our daily lives.

   Discuss any personal concerns that group members are prepared to share regarding faith struggles in their daily lives.

4. What qualities and attitudes will help a person to grow in faith trials rather than break under them? Discuss people you know who are examples of those who have grown through their trials. What did you learn from them?

PART FOUR

FAITH BENEFITS

PREVIEW

The secular media often refer to people who attend church as 'the faithful'. Is that what faith is all about? Doing your duty and turning up to meetings, perhaps praying regularly and doing good deeds in the hope of doing enough to satisfy God? That viewpoint is not even close to the New Testament description of faith. In the life of Jesus and in the other New Testament writings we learn that faith is a daily walk of communion with God. It is filled with many privileges and benefits that become clearer as our faith matures.

So what are some of the features and benefits of living by faith? I raised this question with a number of Christians I know. I include some of their responses along with my own suggestions below.

One of the outstanding benefits is the privilege of walking daily with God. This honour was there at the beginning of creation and we see it surface again in Enoch. Genesis 5:22–24 describes his life in this way:

> After the birth of Methuselah, Enoch lived another 300 years in close fellowship with God, and he had other sons and daughters. Enoch lived 365 years in all. He enjoyed a close relationship with God throughout his life. Then suddenly, he disappeared because God took him.

A living and developing faith will continually desire a closer, more intimate relationship with God. Increasingly He becomes the central focus of our lives. Faith moves us to seek His direction and participation in both the little and the large things that come our way.

Faith moves us closer to the core of our true identity as we allow God to work out His perfect purposes in us and through us. There is great personal satisfaction in finding our true identity and our reason for existence as we trust in and respond to God. Many people have no point of reference for their lives;

no sense of why they exist or what they may become. This is not the experience of those people who have fully embraced the life of faith in God. The life of faith may not always be an easy journey. In fact there are seasons when the pain, tensions and pressures may appear unbearable, but we have someone who is with us always, someone we can turn to for strength, direction and encouragement.

Let's be clear also that a life of faith is not for an elite group of highly gifted or uniquely spiritual people. Each of us is capable of walking closer to God by faith. What Jesus said to His disciples is so encouraging for us. Childlike faith is possible for every person, young or old:

> *One day some parents brought their little children to Jesus so he could touch them and bless them, but the disciples told them not to bother him. Then Jesus called for the children and said to the disciples, "Let the children come to me. Don't stop them! For the Kingdom of God belongs to such as these. I assure you, anyone who doesn't have their kind of faith will never get into the Kingdom of God."*
> (Luke 18:15–17)

A God-focused faith leads us to explore our essential identity. It helps to unfold the core meaning of our lives. There is something very satisfying in finding our true identity and purpose – the reason that God created us in the unique way He has. Living this way will reveal how faithful God is towards us in so many ways. As we become increasingly confident that God is for us always (Rom. 8:35–39) we begin to experience those highly prized qualities: peace of heart and mind, a joy that is far better than happiness, a deep satisfaction, and a more confident hope for both the present and the future.

When our life is based on our faith in God there is a significant overflow into everything we do: bringing up our families, studying or working, balancing our budgets, having fun or working hard, worshipping or wondering, relating to both pleasant and painful people, managing crises and celebrating successes – all we do and all we are.

People with a mature faith are often more effective in overcoming their difficulties because they are not reliant on their own abilities and resources alone but they look to a loving heavenly Father for help (Psa. 121). What a privilege we have to be invited to live this precious life in His faithful presence.

O Lord God Almighty! Where is there anyone as mighty as you, Lord?
Faithfulness is your very character.
(Psa. 89:8)

PERSONAL EXPLORATION

Of all the benefits we have received from God perhaps two of the most remarkable are that God created us in His image to have fellowship with Him, and that even after the human race fell into sin, He was willing to bring us back into right relationship with Him through the death and resurrection of Jesus Christ.

To centre on these two stunning truths we turn to Ephesians 1. This chapter records many of the amazing benefits available to disciples of Jesus Christ. What specific benefits catch your attention in the selections below that are taken from this chapter? Why not jot your thoughts down and spend time reflecting on their significance for you. End your time in thanksgiving to God for His loving kindness towards you.

1. verses 1–8

2. verses 9–14

3. verses 15–18

....

....

....

....

....

....

4. verses 19–23

....

....

....

....

....

....

STUDYING TOGETHER

The key Scripture passage for this session is Psalm 103. In verse 2 the New International Version of the Bible puts it this way: 'Praise the LORD, O my soul, and forget not all his benefits ...'

1. Which of God's benefits to His people in Psalm 103 stands out to you the most at this time? Invite group members to share their choice and explain why they chose it.

....

....

....

....

....

....

2. There are many images or pictures of God in this psalm. Which image captures your attention?

....

....

....

....

....

3. Does King David's view of God appear either surprising or encouraging to you, given his difficult life experiences? What do you believe led him to have such a positive perspective?

4. If you were to choose a verse from this Psalm to encourage yourself for your life situation right now, which one would you choose?

APPLYING THE SCRIPTURES

1. Over the months or years or your Christian experience what are the most obvious blessings you have experienced?

2. God's attitude to our failures and sins is a theme running through this psalm. David is very confident of God's forgiveness and love. Do group members feel the same level of confidence that God has a forgiving and loving attitude towards them?

3. What approach would you take to encourage someone who cannot see
    the benefits of walking with God by faith?

    _____

    _____

    _____

    _____

    _____

    _____

4. Psalm 103 encourages us not to forget God's benefits. As you bring
    this session to a close, why not take time to thank God for some of the
    specific benefits each of you has experienced in your Christian journey.

    _____

    _____

    _____

    _____

    _____

    _____

APPENDIX:

FAITH MYSTERIES

Ask a number of Christians to explain what they understand faith to be and you will find quite a diversity of ideas. Each believer's unique Christian heritage and culture will play a part in shaping their personal understanding of faith, but these ideas undergo continual modification throughout life. Whatever our faith viewpoint, there will always be elements of the life of faith that will surprise us.

There will be other experiences that confuse us. Take for example an actual situation where two people in a local congregation were both diagnosed with cancer that could prove terminal. They both received the same quantity and quality of faithful prayer from many people within the church family who loved them. One died and the other was totally cured, so much so, that even the evidence of chemotherapy disappeared. I know many of us were puzzled and asked all types of answered and unanswerable questions. Faith truly does have its mysteries, which is not really surprising as God speaks through the prophet Isaiah reminding us: 'For my thoughts are not your thoughts, neither are your ways my ways ...' (Isa. 55:8, NIV).

Nevertheless, experiences such as these may spawn a variety of ideas about what faith is and how it works. Here are a few common examples: 'We did not pray hard enough.' 'We did not have enough faith.' 'We should just leave healings and miracles to God and pray, "If it be your will, Father ..."' Other Christians may be so perplexed that they come to believe that prayers of faith are little better than wishful thinking, hoping for the best but always being prepared for the worst.

The first response seems to support the idea that faith is something that we can 'pump up'. If we work hard enough at our faith then God will do what we prayed for. The second approach seems to imply that our prayers don't really have much influence because God is sovereign, He knows the future and He will do whatever He has planned to do, no matter what level of faith we profess. Faith that is no different from wishful thinking is no more than voicing our prayers with little belief or real hope that they will be fulfilled. I don't know about you but somehow these views of faith, and other views like them, don't quite work for me. So what **are** some of the requirements for a strong biblical faith?

KEY ELEMENTS OF A ROBUST FAITH

A biblical understanding of faith

To find greater clarity about the true nature of faith, we need to turn to the Scriptures. This succinct definition of faith found in Hebrews 11:1 is an excellent starting point: 'What is faith? It is the **confident assurance** that what we hope for is going to happen. It is the **evidence** of things we cannot yet see' (emphasis mine). What stands out in these words to me is the importance placed on both confidence and evidence. Faith is not some hazy notion. Biblical faith has substance, it is firmly founded and it has clear objectives in mind.

Faith and relationship with God

A maturing faith requires an increasing level of intimacy with God. Our growing relationship with Him cultivates confidence that God is powerfully involved in all our circumstances no matter how grim they appear from a human perspective. The result is a growing, life-sustaining faith.

The belief element of faith has to do with intellect. The trust element of faith has to do with relationship.

Jesus is Lord of all

A dynamic faith rests on the conviction that Jesus Christ is indeed Lord of all. This includes **every** area of our lives. Each part needs to come under His authority and His direction. We cannot make Him Lord of some areas and not others and expect that our faith will be strong. Are there areas of our lives that are currently not submitted to the lordship of Jesus Christ? These zones that are not surrendered to God put a roadblock in our journey of faith. By holding back certain areas we make a clear statement that God is not allowed into these areas either because we want to keep control of them, or we do not trust Him sufficiently to commit them into His care.

Making the connection between experience and faith

When we turn to the accounts of the ministry of Jesus in the Gospels we find that His teaching and His miracles occurred side by side, each authenticating the other. The combination birthed faith in those who became His disciples. Both components were significant. It is difficult to sustain faith if it is only an intellectual concept or a set of beliefs. Today, a living faith does open our hearts, our minds, and our eyes to the wonders of God at work in His world. These insights invite us to participate in this adventure, to invite Him into the deeper recesses of our lives, and to have our understanding and our obedience stretched beyond our comfort zones. Experiencing God at work strengthens our faith and increases our trust in Him for future challenges.

Persevering faith

A biblical understanding of how God wants to work in this world will produce a persevering faith. This is particularly relevant in the area of prayer. For example, in the early years of the twentieth century a group of Korean Christians met for a long time to pray for God to touch their country. The answer – a major revival – did not occur until the middle of the century, but the unrelenting prayer was greatly rewarded.

Jesus encouraged persevering faith, especially in His parable and teaching in Luke 11:5–13. Surprisingly, sometimes when God's answer to prayer is delayed the intensity of prayer deepens, and strangely, faith may be increased rather than diminished. These prayers of faith take on an edge of desperation and of expectation. In the process the faithful pray-ers become more intimate with the heart of God.

Prayer and fasting

Perhaps the most challenging statement that Jesus made concerning a mature faith is found in the account of the disciples' failure to bring release to the demon possessed child (Mark 9:14–29). They had experienced success in various miraculous areas of ministry previously but their faith was not sufficient for this task. What was missing was a deeper prayer life and possibly, fasting. Jesus recognised the importance of both in His own life. Do we set aside seasons for prayer and fasting in our own lives?

FINAL COMMENTS

It is too easy to live our Christian lives in uncomfortable mediocrity. We can become settled where we are in our Christian journey. This is never a healthy state to be in. There is little satisfaction in spiritual stagnation. Jesus used parables that emphasised the importance of maturing when He talked about the kingdom of God. He used metaphors such as growth (Matt. 13:1–9), pruning (John 15:1–8) and fruitfulness (Luke 6:43–45). Our faith is an essential requirement of this growing process. There is always another level of faith we can explore. There is always more faith-growing we can do.

It is a truly sad state when we become satisfied with less than what God intends for us. None of us has yet reached the level of faith that is possible. God holds out the possibility of so much more. It is my prayer both for you and for me that our faith will continue to grow deeper and become more productive in the coming days and months. We live in a season of history where rapid and uncertain change is everywhere. Our world needs the Church to become all that God intends. This has to start with you and me.

A Christian is a person who confesses that, amidst the manifold and confusing voices heard in the world, there is one Voice which supremely wins his assent, uniting all his powers, intellectual and emotional into a single pattern of self-giving. That voice is Jesus Christ. He (the Christian) believes in Him with all his heart and strength and mind …
[2](Elton Trueblood in *Call of the Committed*).

[2]Quoted by Dr Laura Mae Gardner in *Healthy, Resilient and Effective in Cross Cultural Ministry* (Banding: Percetaken Surya 2013)

You may like to use these pages to journal your thoughts as you explore these issues of faith.

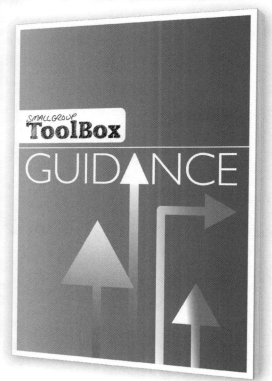

GUIDANCE

This small group study book will
help you set your personal prayers
for guidance firmly within the bigger
plans and purposes of God, something
that can easily be ignored when our
own needs are urgent. *Guidance*
will encourage you to gain a better
Scriptural understanding of what is on
God's heart – the essential foundation
for wise choosing as you make
important life decisions.

48 pages, paperback, 210mm x 148mm
ISBN: 978-1-78259-053-8

Hearing God
ISBN: 978-1-85345-764-7

Discovering Your Spiritual Gifts
ISBN: 978-1-85345-765-4

For current prices visit www.cwr.org.uk/store
Available online or from Christian bookshops

FAITH, HOPE, LOVE AND EVERYTHING IN BETWEEN
By Mick Brooks

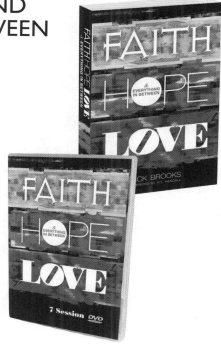

Life is a journey, not a destination!

Although we don't all travel along the journey of discipleship at the same rate, there is a divine pattern at work which, whilst allowing the widest variety for each person and their own individuality, seeks to bring us closer to God through experiences common to us all.

This book and DVD will guide you into a deeper understanding of how the Lord will use every person, circumstance and situation in your life to make you more Christlike.

156 pages, paperback, 230mm x 153mm
Book ISBN: 978-1-85345-598-8
DVD EAN: 5027957-001329

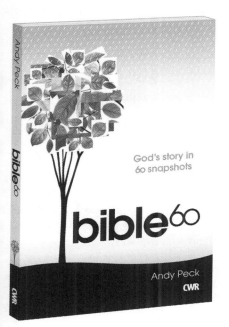

Bible60
By Andy Peck

God's Story in 60 Snapshots

Gain a bigger picture of the whole Bible in only 60 snapshots. Each day includes a key Bible reference, an overview commentary and a 'question to ponder'. Spend just 20 minutes a day for 60 days to discover God's story for yourself. Ideal for individual and church use.

144 pages, paperback, 197mm x 129mm
ISBN: 978-1-85345-923-8

For current prices visit www.cwr.org.uk/store
Available online or from Christian bookshops

Courses and seminars

Publishing and media

Conference facilities

Transforming lives

CWR's vision is to enable people to experience personal transformation through applying God's Word to their lives and relationships.

Our Bible-based training and resources help people around the world to:
• Grow in their walk with God
• Understand and apply Scripture to their lives
• Equip themselves and their church
• Develop pastoral care and counselling skills
• Train for leadership
• Strengthen relationships, marriage and family life and much more.

Our insightful writers provide daily Bible-reading notes and other resources for all ages, and our course presenters have gained an international reputation for excellence and effectiveness.

CWR's Training and Conference Centres in Surrey and East Sussex, England, provide distinguished facilities in idyllic settings – ideal for both learning and spiritual refreshment.

CWR Applying God's Word
to everyday life and relationships

CWR, Waverley Abbey House,
Waverley Lane, Farnham,
Surrey GU9 8EP, UK

Telephone: **+44 (0)1252 784700**
Email: **info@cwr.org.uk**
Website: **www.cwr.org.uk**

Registered Charity No 294387
Company Registration No 1990308